# Birds *of* Prey
## An Introduction

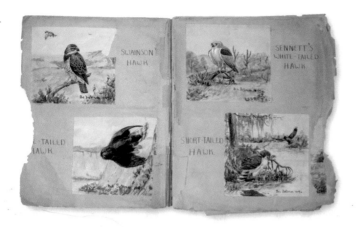

(Above) *Hawks of North America*, Robert Bateman, age 14

ISBN-10: 1-897330-12-X
ISBN-13: 978-1-897330-12-8

This Scholastic edition is only available for distribution through the school market.

Printed in Singapore by Tien Wah Press

# Birds of Prey

## An Introduction

### Robert Bateman

#### with Nancy Kovacs

A Scholastic / Madison Press Book

# Riveted by Raptors

Wherever I have traveled in the world, birds of prey have starred in some of my most thrilling memories. Once, when I was hiking in the mountains, I came upon a silver-furred hoary marmot. To my delight, it was unconcerned by my presence. But as I watched, it suddenly became alarmed, shrieking its whistling cry. At the same moment I heard a roaring noise, like a distant jet, as a Golden Eagle zoomed down from the sky toward the marmot's perch. The marmot dived into its burrow, safe. The Eagle, thwarted in its quest for food, swerved and flew away.

We often think of birds of prey, or raptors, in human terms. We see eagles as symbols of strength. Hawks and falcons represent ferocity. Owls are symbols of wisdom in some cultures, because their faces look so human. The very word "vulture" brings to mind a vivid picture of greed. But raptors are not a part of the human world. They are wild animals with an important job. They kill other animals for food, and by doing so they help to control the populations of their prey.

Where can you find raptors? Look out your car window on a country drive, and you may spot a hawk perched in a tree. Lie on your back in a field on a warm autumn day, and you may see hawks or vultures circling high overhead. Search among the trees in a wood, and you may find an owl resting on a branch.

This book is an introduction to some of my favorite raptors. I hope it will start you on your own journey to discover these amazing birds.

## Golden Eagle

**Length:** 33–38" / 84–97 cm

**Wingspan:** 7' / 2.1 m

**Weight:** Male 8–10 lbs / 3.6–4.5 kg;
female 9–12.5 lbs / 4–5.7 kg

**Food:** Small to medium-sized mammals,
grouse, pigeons, snakes, turtles, some
carrion

**Range:** Throughout North America,
Asia, North Africa

**Migration:** Short- to medium-
distance, partial migration

**Habitat:** Mountainous regions

# What is a Bird of Prey?

*Eagle flew down from his perch, seized a lamb, and carried it off in his talons. Crow, who was watching, was jealous and decided to imitate the strength and flight of Eagle. With a great whir of his wings, he settled on a large ram, but his claws became tangled in the fleece. He could not free himself, although he fluttered his wings as hard as he could. The shepherd, seeing Crow, ran up and caught him. He clipped Crow's wings and gave him to his children. When they asked, "Father, what kind of bird is it?" he replied, "I am certain he is a crow, but he wishes he were an eagle."*

*— adapted from Aesop's Fables*

From the earliest times, birds of prey have been the subject of story and legend. Images of Snowy Owls have been found in cave paintings in Europe. In ancient Egypt, the hieroglyph for the letter "A" was an eagle or vulture, and "M" was an owl. Admired by many and feared by some, birds of prey are among the most exciting creatures on Earth.

They are found everywhere on the planet, except Antarctica, and in every type of habitat. They live in forests, mountains, rainforests, and deserts. This Elf Owl (below) makes its desert home in old woodpecker nests, often in saguaro cactuses. The Rough-legged Hawk, on the other hand, breeds in the far north, migrating south in the wintertime.

Many birds catch and eat live prey, so how are raptors special? They have keen eyesight. Their curved, sharp beaks can tear tough tendons and muscles. Their strong feet have long, sharp talons for grasping and carrying their prey. Their wings and tails give them swift flight and agility. They are perfectly designed for hunting.

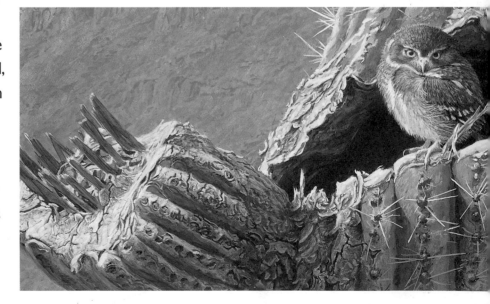

# The Types of Birds of Prey

Birds of prey are divided into two groups: hawks and owls. Hawks are further divided into the following groups, known as families: Buteos, Accipiters, Eagles, Falcons, Kites, Ospreys, Secretary Birds, and Vultures.

## Buteos (*bew-tay-ohs*)

There are more species of Buteos than any other type of hawk. Their tails are fairly short, and their wings are long. They often soar above the ground, but they also hunt from perches on trees or posts.

## Accipiters (*axe-ip-it-ers*)

Accipiter hawks are known for their "flap-flap-flap, glide" flight pattern. With shorter wings and longer tails than Buteos, they are very agile fliers, but slower. They often hunt through thick, tangled woods, and are rarely seen soaring.

## Eagles

Eagles are the largest hawks. Myths tell of eagles stealing young children, and scientists have recently discovered that a large ancestor of the African Crowned Eagle did exactly that some two or three million years ago. Today's eagles are very shy of humans, though, and are not strong enough to fly away with a child.

## Falcons

Swift and agile, they can change direction in a heartbeat and drop from the sky onto their prey at incredible speeds.

## Kites

These light, beautiful hawks live in warm habitats and dine on insects, reptiles, amphibians, and snails. They are graceful and acrobatic in flight.

## Ospreys

The Osprey is the sole species in its family. It eats only fish. The Osprey goes completely underwater to catch its prey, and then it carries the fish headfirst to its perch.

## Secretary Birds

The Secretary Bird is also the only species in its family and is like no other bird of prey. It runs after snakes and small animals on its unusually long legs. It kills by stamping on prey with its powerful feet.

## Vultures

Vultures are divided into Old World and New World types. Old World vultures are members of the hawk family. New World vultures are more closely related to storks, but have always been considered birds of prey because they look like Old World vultures and eat carrion.

## Owls

With their concave, dish-shaped faces and forward-facing eyes, owls have a solemn appearance that makes them seem wise. But owls are probably no wiser than any other bird.

# Red-shouldered Hawk and Augur Buzzard

The Red-shouldered Hawk can drop down onto its prey or hunt on the ground by hopping after small animals. It does not like to share territory with other raptors, but it is not very shy of humans. It's one of the most vocal birds of prey and its loud, whistling "kee-ahh" call, repeated several times, may be heard resounding through its woodland home.

Red-shouldered Hawks and American Crows sometimes try to steal each other's food. Occasionally the two enemies will join forces to heckle a Great Horned Owl in their territory.

The beautiful Augur Buzzard is very common in the highlands of Africa. It hunts both from a perch and from the sky. Hanging motionless in the air, it rides the strong winds coming off a hilltop. It attacks from this hover by dropping straight down onto its prey.

### Red-shouldered Hawk

**Length:** 17–24" / 43–61 cm

**Wingspan:** 23.5–50" / 60–127 cm

**Weight:** Male 19 oz / 0.5 kg; female 25 oz / 0.7 kg

**Food:** Small mammals, some birds, reptiles, insects, amphibians, spiders, invertebrates

**Range:** U.S. and southern Canada

**Migration:** Usually migrates only from northern part of range

**Habitat:** Swamps, wooded wetlands

### Augur Buzzard

**Length:** 19.7–22.4" / 50–57 cm

**Wingspan:** 4.5' / 1.3 m

**Food:** Small ground mammals, snakes, lizards, small ground birds, insects, roadkill carrion

**Range:** Somalia, Ethiopia, west through southern Sudan and Uganda to eastern Democratic Republic of Congo

**Habitat:** Mountain ranges, hilly woodlands, open savanna, forest, plains

Robert Bateman.

# Northern Goshawk

**Length:** 19–27" / 48–69 cm

**Wingspan:** 40–47" / 1–1.2 m

**Weight:** Male 1.5–3 lbs / 0.7–1.4 kg; female 1.3–3.5 lbs / 0.6–1.6 kg

**Food:** Small mammals, medium-sized birds, grasshoppers, some moth and beetle larvae

**Range:** North America, Europe, Asia from northern timberline to subtropics

**Migration:** Partial migrant; some are resident year-round

**Habitat:** Forests, mountains

# Northern Goshawk and Sharp-shinned Hawk

The Northern Goshawk is a large, fierce woodland bird. It is especially fond of Ruffed Grouse, a game bird found in the woods. Once it spots its prey, the Goshawk darts around trees and shrubs with remarkable agility and determination, its red eyes gleaming. When it gets close, the Goshawk drops suddenly, piercing the bird or animal with its sharp talons and killing it instantly. Even if the prey manages to hide, the Goshawk will go right after it, tearing away at obstacles like leaves or small branches, risking injury to itself in the process.

Admired for its strength and ferocity, the Goshawk has long been a favorite for the sport of falconry. A Goshawk's image decorated the helmet of European conqueror Attila the Hun sixteen hundred years ago.

Like all Accipiters, the small Sharp-shinned Hawk flies skillfully and can navigate thick woods with ease. Its thin, flat-sided legs account for its funny name. It prefers to hunt small songbirds close to its own size, such as the Varied Thrush (below), snatching them out of the air with its sharp claws. The female "Sharpie," nearly twice as large as the male, eats far more than her partner. She can consume up to three small birds at one meal.

## Sharp-shinned Hawk

**Length:** 10–14" / 25–36 cm

**Wingspan:** 20–27" / 51–69 cm

**Food:** Small birds, young chickens; will attack larger birds

**Range:** Alaska and northern Canada to southern U.S., Mexico and Panama; Bahamas

**Habitat:** Large, remote woods

## Bald Eagle

**Length:** 34–43" / 86–109 cm

**Wingspan:** 6–7.5' / 1.8–2.3 m

**Weight:** Male 8–9 lbs / 3.6–4 kg; female 10–14 lbs / 4.5–6.4 kg

**Food:** Fish, weakened waterfowl, rodents, carrion

**Range:** North America, northeastern Siberia

**Migration:** As needed, following its food supply

**Habitat:** Usually near water; mountain ridges when migrating

# Bald Eagle and
# African Fish Eagle

The majestic Bald Eagle is the second-largest bird of prey in North America — only the California Condor is larger. Despite its name, this eagle isn't really bald. "Bald" comes from *balde*, which meant "white" in Old English.

Bald Eagles are most often found near water, looking for their favorite food: fish. They hunt, but these giants also eat carrion and steal from other raptors. They will even tackle the large Osprey, snatching a fresh catch right out of its talons.

Bald Eagles nearly disappeared in eastern regions of North America because of the use of the pesticide DDT. It has now been banned, and the Eagles are becoming more common.

The African Fish Eagle is closely related to the Bald Eagle, and I think it is a more striking-looking bird. The African Fish Eagle does not scavenge, but catches and eats only fresh fish. Its clear, brilliant yodeling call has earned it the nickname "The Voice of Africa." While calling, it has the distinctive habit of throwing its head way back and then forward again.

### African Fish Eagle

**Length:** 25–29" / 64–74 cm

**Wingspan:** 6–8' / 1.8–2.5 m

**Food:** Fish

**Range:** Africa, south of the Sahara

**Habitat:** Near rivers, lakes, and coasts

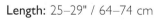

# Martial Eagle and African Black Eagle

A ferocious giant, the Martial Eagle flies so high that it is hard to see with the naked eye. Soaring overhead for hours each day, it perches in early morning or early evening. These are the best times to see it.

Although they can kill the young of large animals, such as the impala, Martial Eagles prefer smaller animals. I once saw one swoop down on a group of banded mongooses. The shadow it cast was huge, and the mongooses ran quickly into cover — not quickly enough, though. The Eagle stretched out its long legs and claws, seized one mongoose by the head, and carried it off to a distant tree.

The African Black Eagle, also called Verreaux's Eagle, is a magnificent bird of canyons, escarpments, and cliffs. It has bold, white markings on its back and under its wings, and loves to feast on the rock-hyrax, a small, furry mammal that looks like a rodent, but is more closely related to elephants.

Black Eagles always take their prey on the ground, plunging down without warning to make their kill. They are not the most aggressive raptors, but are known to attack large animals, like leopards, to defend their nests.

## African Black Eagle

**Length:** 31.5–37" / 80–94 cm

**Wingspan:** up to 8' / 2.5 m

**Food:** Rock-hyrax and other mammals, including young antelopes, lambs, baboons, hares

**Range:** Eastern and southern Africa

**Habitat:** Mountainous areas

## Martial Eagle

**Length:** 31–34" / 79–86 cm

**Wingspan:** up to 8' / 2.5 m

**Weight:** Male 11 lbs / 5 kg; female 13 lbs / 6 kg

**Food:** Rock-hyrax and other mammals, including small antelopes, jackals, and baboons

**Range:** Africa, south of the Sahara, especially in the east

**Migration:** Year-round resident

**Habitat:** Mainly savanna, from desert to forest edge; open wooded country

# Senses for Survival

We rely on our five senses — sight, hearing, smell, taste, and touch — to survive. Do birds of prey use the same senses? The answer is that they do, but they use them differently.

## Sight

Birds have phenomenal eyesight. Their eyes are much larger than ours, compared to the size of their heads, and they can see better than we can. They don't see *more* than we do, but they are able to pick out details better and faster. When you watch a baseball pitcher throw a ball, the ball is a blur. A bird like the Golden Eagle (below) would not only see the ball clearly, but would also take in the fans in the stands, the umpire, the players, and the mice under the dugout benches. It would see all of this instantly — and with great accuracy.

All birds see in color, but kestrels have an extra advantage — they can see ultraviolet light. This helps them find voles, whose urine reflects ultraviolet. Kestrels also have dark vertical lines on their cheeks, just like the black stuff football players apply under their eyes. These lines absorb any blinding sunlight that might interfere with kestrels' sight.

Hawks' eyes are set farther forward than other birds', so they don't see as well at the sides — but their forward vision is excellent. Owls are similar. With eyes set in dish-shaped faces, they have exceptional forward vision but no real side vision. To make up for this limited range, their necks are very flexible and can rotate almost all the way around. They do this so quickly that people often think their heads turn completely around. If they did that, though, their necks would break!

## Hearing

Birds hear through ear openings at the sides of their heads. Usually these openings are covered with feathers. Vultures, though, have no feathers on their heads, so we can see their ear openings clearly.

As far as scientists can tell, a bird's sense of hearing is not better than that of a human. A nocturnal owl like this Great Horned Owl, though, often relies on its sense of hearing to locate prey in the dark. The placement of each of its ears in a slightly different spot on either side of its head allows it to pinpoint the origin of a noise with great accuracy.

## Touch

Birds are very sensitive to being touched on their feathers because of special nerve endings at the bases of their wing and tail feathers. Many birds have nerve endings in their tongues and palates that help them find food. Birds of prey also use their beaks to feel things, which no doubt aids them in eating.

## Taste

Birds don't have many taste buds and, since they have no teeth, they don't chew. Instead, birds like the Tawny Eagle and two Egyptian Vultures in this painting (opposite, top) swallow their food quickly. In spite of this, some use a sense of taste to help them select the food they like. One researcher tested a captive Barred Owl's sense of taste by feeding it a toad one day instead of its usual frog. The owl took the toad in its mouth then spat it out — likely because of the poison a toad's skin gives off when it is disturbed. The owl never accepted a toad again and even stopped eating frogs, probably because they looked like toads. Both falcons and owls will reject food if it is not fresh.

## Smell

Most birds of prey probably can't smell very much at all, but a biologist friend told me an interesting story about Turkey Vultures and a gas pipeline. The pipeline had sprung a leak and the engineers were having trouble finding it. Natural gas has no odor, so they added a chemical to the gas that made it smell like rotting

food. Soon, a group of Turkey Vultures like this one (right) were attracted by the smell and they gathered at the site of the leak, expecting to find a meal. The engineers then simply followed the circling birds to the leak.

King Vultures have a fairly strong sense of smell, too. Black Vultures and Condors don't, but they watch Turkey and King Vultures and follow them to food.

## Peregrine Falcon

**Length:** 15–20" / 38–51 cm

**Wingspan:** 43–46" / 1.1–1.2 m

**Weight:** Male 1.3–1.8 lbs / 0.6–0.8 kg; female 2–3 lbs / 0.9–1.4 kg

**Food:** Small birds, occasionally mammals, large insects

**Range:** Every continent except Antarctica

**Migration:** Northern birds fly south to warm climates; southern birds move short distances

**Habitat:** Open country around rocky cliffs; ocean and bay coastlines, bridges, water towers, cities

# Peregrine Falcon and Pygmy Falcon

Peregrine Falcons are amazingly talented flyers — in fact, they may be the fastest birds in the world. These feathered rockets can reach speeds of at least fifty miles (eighty kilometers) per hour. They prey mostly on other birds. When a Peregrine spots prey, it plunges, knocks the bird on the head with its sharp talons, then carries the unconscious bird to its perch. Sometimes a Peregrine will pass the bird to its mate in mid-air. The female flies underneath and turns upside-down to take the captured prey from the male.

In the 1950s, the number of Peregrines decreased alarmingly due to pesticide use. Efforts to save this extraordinary bird have been successful, thanks to captive breeding and the banning of DDT. Peregrines are now often seen nesting in tall buildings in cities, where there is a plentiful supply of pigeons to eat.

The African Pygmy Falcon is about the size of an American Robin. Its soft feathers and fluffy appearance hide the fact that it is a ruthless hunter of smaller birds and insects. It takes over the abandoned nests of a bird called the White-headed Buffalo Weaver, and this little raptor's aggressive behavior keeps predators away from other weaver birds nesting in the same area.

## Pygmy Falcon

**Length:** 7–8" / 18–20 cm

**Wingspan:** 15" / 38 cm

**Food:** Large insects, small lizards, some small rodents and birds

**Range:** East Africa

**Habitat:** Dry, open bush; wooded areas up to 5,250' / 1,600 m above sea level

# Gyrfalcon and American Kestrel

The Arctic is rich with beautiful wildlife, but none is more spectacular than the Gyrfalcon (*jurr-falcon*). Its fierce expression conveys dignity and strength. This largest of all falcons is found in three color variations: black, gray, or white. In each variation its feathers are streaked and stippled with contrasting color patterns.

While hunting, the Gyrfalcon will rocket straight up to a bird flying overhead and strike from below with its feet — usually breaking the bird's breastbone. Or it may drive its prey to the ground before killing it.

The strikingly elegant American Kestrel is the smallest falcon in North America. It is a tiny aristocrat, compact and graceful. It separates the feathers at the ends of its wings to make its flight smooth and silent. The Kestrel hunts mostly in the morning and late afternoon, but during the day you may see it perched on a wire, its tail moving up and down.

## Gyrfalcon

**Length:** 20–25" / 51–64 cm

**Wingspan:** 48–54" / 1.2–1.4 m

**Weight:** Male 2–3 lbs / 0.9–1.4 kg; female 2.5–4.5 lbs / 1.1–2 kg

**Food:** Birds, especially Arctic ptarmigans; some small mammals

**Range:** Northern regions of Northern Hemisphere

**Migration:** Only northernmost residents migrate

**Habitat:** Marshes, open country, foothill tundra, mountains, sea cliffs, river bluffs, nests on cliff ledges

## American Kestrel

**Length:** 9–12" / 23–30 cm

**Wingspan:** 20–24.5" / 51–62 cm

**Food:** Insects, bats, mice, birds, lizards, small snakes, frogs

**Range:** Northern North America through Mexico, West Indies, and South America

**Habitat:** Woodland borders, open fields, highways, arid plains, deserts

# Flight and Feathers

**B**irds are the only creatures in the animal kingdom to have feathers. Feathers protect birds from heat and cold and allow water to slide off their bodies, which is useful to water birds like the Osprey (below). Feathers can also shift and rotate slightly to help with flight, they can fluff up to shield against the wind, and they add color and ornaments such as crests and long tails.

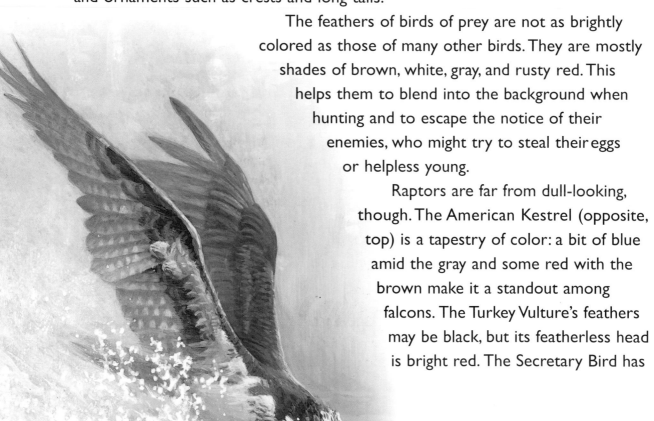

The feathers of birds of prey are not as brightly colored as those of many other birds. They are mostly shades of brown, white, gray, and rusty red. This helps them to blend into the background when hunting and to escape the notice of their enemies, who might try to steal their eggs or helpless young.

Raptors are far from dull-looking, though. The American Kestrel (opposite, top) is a tapestry of color: a bit of blue amid the gray and some red with the brown make it a standout among falcons. The Turkey Vulture's feathers may be black, but its featherless head is bright red. The Secretary Bird has a showy crest, and the Snowy Owl's dark-spotted white plumage looks like the softest ermine. The Harris's Hawk appears to be solidly dark brown, but there are patches of reddish-brown on its wings and legs, and its tail is edged in a white that flashes when it flies.

Raptors are the flight specialists of the bird world. Many hawks and vultures soar to search for food. The California Condor (opposite, top) can stay aloft for hours on air currents high above the ground, hardly ever flapping its wings. Falcons use their short wings and long tails to fly quickly and steer accurately through woods or around buildings.

The flight wings of owls, like the Barn Owl (left), are lined with very soft, saw-toothed feathers. This makes their flight silent, so they can clearly hear their prey and quietly approach, giving hunted animals little chance of escape.

# Black Kite

**Length:** 22–24" / 55–60 cm

**Wingspan:** 51–61" / 1.3–1.6 m

**Weight:** 12.4–26.5 lbs / 0.6–1.2 kg

**Food:** Lizards, small mammals, insects, carrion

**Range:** Australia, Africa, Asia, Europe

**Migration:** Moves to warmer climates in winter; some year-round residents

**Habitat:** A variety of habitats, including fields, plains, meadows, and near water

# Black Kite and Swallow-tailed Kite

Black Kites are the world's most common raptor. They cover a huge range of territory, live in a variety of habitats, and are very tolerant of people. I saw these black kites (opposite) at the sixteenth-century City Palace in Udaipur, northern India, where they often steal food that has been left as an offering to the gods.

The light weight of the Black Kite allows it to take to the sky earlier in the day than heavier birds, which need warmer air currents to gain soaring altitude. Black Kites eat insects as they fly and often circle in large flocks, which is unusual for raptors. In Australia, a flock of thousands was once seen soaring above a pig farm.

The Swallow-tailed Kite is in the air most of the day, except when it rains. Beautiful and graceful, with a long, deeply forked, swallow-like tail, this black and white hawk seems to dominate the sky. It rarely flaps its wings, but rotates its tail to turn or maintain direction.

Rather than land to catch its prey, the Swallow-tailed Kite will often fly low over vegetation, capturing large insects in its talons as it goes. It can also drink on the fly, skimming the surface of the water.

## Swallow-tailed Kite

**Length:** 19–25.5" / 48–65 cm

**Wingspan:** 45–50" / 1.1–1.2 m

**Food:** Insects, small snakes, lizards, frogs, small birds

**Range:** Southern U.S., Mexico, Central and South America

**Habitat:** Swamps, marshes, along rivers, ponds and lakes, open forest

# Osprey and Secretary Bird

The Osprey is one of the world's best-known birds of prey. It dives feet-first and wings-up into the water, disappearing in the spray, to grasp its prey. When it emerges, the Osprey carries the fish to its perch, holding it head-forward to reduce air resistance. The Osprey's claws are barbed underneath, which helps it hold on to slippery fish. It shakes water from its feathers on the fly. When it is wet, the disheveled feathers give the Osprey a somewhat demented look, but it is one of the most thrilling birds of prey to watch in action.

With its very long legs and short claws, the Secretary Bird doesn't look like a bird of prey at all. It can fly gracefully, but it hunts mainly on the ground, using its lanky legs to run down its prey. Snakes are this bird's favorite food. When it sees one, it pounces, gives a hard kick with its powerful feet, and deals the death blow with its blunt rear talon.

The Secretary Bird got its name in the 1800s. The secretaries of the time used to tuck their quill pens behind their ears. The quills would stick out like the feathers on a Secretary Bird's head.

## Secretary Bird

**Length:** 55" / 140 cm

**Wingspan:** 6.5–7.1' / 2–2.2 m

**Food:** Snakes, other reptiles, small mammals, young birds and eggs

**Range:** Africa, south of the Sahara

**Habitat:** Savanna and open grassland

## Osprey

**Length:** 20–25" / 51–63.5 cm

**Wingspan:** 54–72" / 1.3–1.8 m

**Weight:** Male 2.6–3.6 lbs / 1.1–1.6 kg; female 2.8–4.5 lbs / 1.2–2 kg

**Food:** Freshwater and saltwater fish

**Range:** Worldwide, except Antarctica

**Migration:** Northern populations migrate to warmer climates

**Habitat:** Along lakes, rivers, seacoasts

# Beaks and Talons

How do you identify an unknown bird? The first things to take note of are its size, shape, and the way it flies or perches.

A thick beak for breaking seeds means it's some sort of finch. A long, thin beak is the sign of a hummingbird. What helps you identify a bird of prey like this Red-tailed Hawk (right)? Look at its beak and its talons. They're the tools that these hunters need to make their catch. All their other highly developed skills — their eyesight and hearing, the way they fly — would be useless without their special beaks and talons.

## Beaks

The sharp, hooked beak of a raptor such as this Gyrfalcon (left) is a multipurpose tool. The beak can feel, carry food and nest materials, and tear at the flesh of a freshly killed animal. The upper part of the beak, near the face, is soft and dense. This allows the bird to open its mouth wider, giving it greater flexibility for eating.

The beak of each species is specially designed for that bird's needs. For example, the Short-eared Owl's beak is strong enough to kill a small animal with a bite at the back of its skull. Its beak can open wide enough to swallow the animal whole. Most vultures have weak beaks and cannot tear fresh meat. They wait until the meat has rotted and become softer.

## Feet and Talons

Hawks and owls have feet armed with long, sharp toes called talons. They use their talons to seize prey, carry it to a perch, and tear it open.

The Burrowing Owl uses its long legs and feet to dig out its burrow. It often hunts by running along the ground to search for insects and small animals, capturing them in its talons.

Birds, including raptors, have three toes pointing forward and one backward, but there are a couple of exceptions. Ospreys' toes are arranged two forward and two backward — no doubt this helps them carry their fish. Owls can rotate their outer toe from front to back. I painted this Verreaux's Eagle Owl (right) perched on a branch with two toes in front and two back.

# Lammergeier and White-backed Vulture

The Lammergeier (*lam-er-guy-er*), a regal-looking vulture of mountains and cliffs, has a distinctive black mask and beardlike feathers on its chin. It soars overhead looking for food and nests, and it raises its young on sheltered ledges. One magical morning in the Spanish Pyrenees, I was directed to a cliff where a Lammergeier was nesting. When my companions and I arrived there, we could see a half-grown chick on the nest, trying its wings. We watched until a shadow fell over the cliff and one of the parents, its golden neck ruff glowing in the sun, flew down to feed its young.

The Lammergeier is famous for the way it gets the marrow out of bones. First, it carries the bone up as high as 200 feet (60 meters) above the ground and drops it onto a rock below. The Lammergeier repeats this until the bone finally cracks, exposing the marrow. Then the bird gobbles it up — marrow, broken bone, and all. Its digestive system dissolves the bone and absorbs the marrow.

The White-backed Vulture finds carrion by following smaller vultures that soar lower in the sky. When it spreads its wings to follow them, the distinctive white markings on its back are visible to higher-flying vultures, who in turn join the parade to the carrion. Eventually, there may be as many as 200 vultures at one dead animal, cleaning the carcass in just an hour!

## White-backed Vulture

**Length:** 37" / 95 cm

**Wingspan:** 6.5' / 2 m

**Food:** Carrion, locusts, termites

**Range:** South of the Sahara to South Africa

**Habitat:** Savanna and open woodland

## Lammergeier

**Length:** 43" / 110 cm

**Wingspan:** 9' / 2.7 m

**Weight:** Up to 17 lbs / 7.7 kg

**Food:** Carrion, especially the internal organs; turtles, small mammals, small birds, bones, bone marrow

**Range:** Asia, southern Europe, northern Africa

**Migration:** Year-round resident

**Habitat:** Remote, mountainous areas; cliff ledges

# Turkey Vulture and King Vulture

When I was living in southern Ontario, I used to watch for the Turkey Vultures' return in the spring. In those days, they were less common than they are now, and the sight of them perched in their classic vulture pose, waiting for the day to warm up, was always fascinating. Some may not find vultures handsome, but in the air they are truly beautiful. With wings held in a distinctive "V" shape, they can stay aloft for hours, slowly tilting from side to side high above the earth. Their incredible sense of smell allows them to find carrion far below.

All vultures have interesting ways to protect themselves from dangerous bacteria. Their featherless heads are easily cleaned after a feast of rotting food, and special enzymes in their stomachs break down bacteria. Turkey Vultures have an extra defense: they urinate on their legs. The acids in their urine destroy the bacteria they pick up while walking in their decaying food.

The bright color of King Vultures helps them find one another in the forests where they live. They soar high over the jungle, as many as ten at a time, searching for carrion below. Because they are larger and have stronger beaks than other vultures, they can kill their rivals, so they are given the first chance at a carcass. Their weaker vulture cousins must wait and eat what the King Vultures leave behind.

## King Vulture

**Length:** 28–32" / 71–81 cm

**Wingspan:** 6.5' / 2 m

**Food:** Carrion of all kinds; reported to kill live reptiles, calves

**Range:** Southern Mexico, Central and South America

**Habitat:** Forests

## Turkey Vulture

**Length:** 26–32" / 66–81 cm

**Wingspan:** 68–72" / 1.7–1.8 m

**Weight:** 4.5–5 lbs / 2–2.2 kg (female slightly larger)

**Food:** Fresh to putrid carrion of all kinds

**Range:** Southern Canada to southern South America; Bahamas, West Indies

**Migration:** Northernmost birds migrate south in winter

**Habitat:** Open plains, desert, forest, jungle

# Snowy Owl and Barn Owl

**N**early every winter for as long as I can remember, I've seen Snowy Owls that have migrated south from their Arctic breeding grounds. Unlike other owls, these beautiful white birds are daytime hunters. Their acute sense of hearing allows them to find prey even in dense grass or deep snow. In the Arctic, their favorite food is lemmings, little hamster-like mammals that live in burrows of snow.

Once, I was watching a Snowy Owl in a field, binoculars to my eyes. It made eye contact, staring steadily at me for a few moments with its round, yellow eyes. If this ever happens to you, you will never forget the thrill!

Barn Owls are known for their heart-shaped faces and for their habit of roosting during the day in barns, caves, tree cavities, and other secluded places. They hunt at night, flying silently over the fields in search of small animals. Their sense of hearing is among the best in the animal kingdom.

## Snowy Owl

**Length:** 20–27" / 51–69 cm

**Wingspan:** 54–66" / 1.3–1.6 m

**Weight:** Male 3–4 lbs / 1.4–1.8 kg; females 4–6 lbs / 1.8–2.7 kg

**Food:** Lemmings, mice, birds, fish, marine animals

**Range:** Arctic regions

**Migration:** Follows food sources as necessary, as far as southern Canada and northern U.S.

**Habitat:** Tundra, barren grounds

## Barn Owl

**Length:** 14–20" / 35–51 cm

**Wingspan:** 43–47" / 1–1.1 m

**Food:** Small mammals, some birds

**Range:** North America, Eurasia, Africa

**Habitat:** Meadows, fields, towns, farms (sometimes nests in barn lofts)

# Tawny Owl and
# Screech Owl

The Tawny Owl has all-black eyes and no ear tufts. It is plump and gray to reddish-brown. At night, it perches in a tree, listening. When it hears its prey, it glides on silent wings through the woods. Swooping down, the Tawny Owl covers the animal with its wings, then kills it instantly with a blow from its feet and talons. During the day, the Tawny Owl perches on a branch and presses itself close to the trunk, especially if songbirds in the area have spotted it and sent out alarm calls.

If you see a young Tawny Owl outside its nest cavity, don't approach. The mother might attack you, thinking that you are a predator.

My friends and I used to haunt the orchards near Toronto looking for Screech Owls. We would check tree cavities, hoping to find them hiding there, and try to lure them out. Sometimes they would be perched in a tree nearby, their color blending in with the bark, and we would see them only as we were leaving. This small North American owl doesn't really screech. It has two common calls. One, called the Bounce Song, is a whistled, hooting trill on one note. The other, a territorial call, is its rather ghostly, downward trilling "hoooooo." Some people think the sound is eerie, but I find it pleasant and soothing.

## Screech Owl

**Length:** 7–10" / 18–25 cm

**Wingspan:** 18–24" / 46–61 cm

**Food:** Mice, shrews, other mammals, insects, small reptiles, amphibians

**Range:** Southeast Alaska, southern Canada, U.S. into Mexico

**Habitat:** Villages, woodlots, old orchards, wooded canyons, giant-cactus country

## Tawny Owl

**Length:** 14.5–17" / 37–43 cm

**Wingspan:** 32–38" / 81–96 cm

**Weight:** Male 10.6–19.4 oz / 300–650 g; female 14.5–28.2 oz / 410–800 g

**Food:** Rodents, small birds

**Range:** Europe, North Africa, parts of Asia

**Migration:** Year-round resident

**Habitat:** Deciduous woodland, farms, parks, large gardens

# Family Life

The key to survival for all living things is the care of their young. Fierce and relentless as hunters, birds of prey are like all birds when it comes to nesting. They must provide food and protection until their young are old enough and strong enough to fend for themselves. Since they develop fairly slowly, raptor young must be protected and fed longer than most other birds.

## Mating

Most birds of prey mate for life. The male courts the female by displaying his flying ability, sometimes feeding the female as part of the ritual. The more food he brings her during courtship, the more certain she is that he will take good care of her and their young.

## Nests

Many birds of prey nest in high places, like trees and cliffs, even platforms provided by humans. Ospreys (above) will often make use of such platforms, and their nests are amazing feats of engineering. The males carry the materials to the nest site, and the females do the building. Large branches form the bottom, and smaller branches and vegetation fill out the nest. Flat materials — even plastic bags — line the nest so that the eggs won't fall through any cracks. Ospreys use the same nest year after year, adding to it and repairing it as needed.

## Eggs and Hatching

Birds of prey lay their eggs sometimes as early as late winter, so their chicks hatch at the beginning of spring. Hawks lay as many as four eggs at a time, which they incubate for up to eight weeks. The larger the eggs, the longer they take to incubate. The female tends the eggs, while the male hunts and feeds both himself and his mate. Later, he brings food for the nestlings as well. The only tooth a bird ever has is its egg tooth, which it uses to break open its shell. The tooth falls off after hatching.

Once hatched, young birds can be very competitive. Barn Owls sometimes lay more than eight eggs over the course of several days. In years when food is scarce, the chicks that hatch later are too small to compete for food, and they die. The older chicks will often eat their dead nest-mates.

## Young and Fledglings

Raptors are helpless at birth. They must be cared for until they can fly and hunt for themselves, often many weeks after hatching. Northern Goshawks are especially fierce in protecting their young, sometimes attacking passing hikers with their sharp claws.

When young Ospreys (right) are nearly ready to leave the nest, they stand at the edge of the nest, flexing and flapping their wings. If they try to fly before they are ready and fall to the ground, their chances of survival are very slim.

# Other Hunters

**B**irds of prey may be the best-known hunters in the bird world, but they aren't the only ones. Many birds — flycatchers, for instance, and even hummingbirds — eat insects. Robins eat worms. Many wading birds, like Great Blue Herons (opposite, right), eat fish, frogs, and even small mammals they find along the shore.

Loggerhead Shrikes (left) are carnivorous songbirds. They have short, hooked bills, their legs and feet are very strong, and their sharp claws are adapted for grasping their prey. They eat insects, small reptiles, mammals, and small or nesting birds. Like a raptor, a Shrike will swoop down to carry off its prey, which it kills with a strike of the sturdy notch at the tip of its bill. A Shrike's feet and talons aren't as strong as a raptor's, though. So it spears its catch on a thorn, stem, or the metal barb of a fence, or wedges it in the fork of a branch to eat it or store it for a while.

Nighthawks are not hawks at all. They belong to a family of birds that includes the whippoorwill. They live on insects, usually caught in flight at night or twilight. You often hear their buzzing call as they fly around streetlights or near the lights over sports stadiums, where insects congregate at night. The Common Nighthawk is typical of these birds, with its mottled feathers, whiskered face, and short, curved bill.

Even vultures are given a run for their money by other birds. Both Crows and Ravens are omnivorous, eating meat, grain, fruit, garbage, and carrion. You often see them on the road, eating an animal that has been hit by a car.

King Penguins (below) hunt underwater for their meals of fish, squid, and krill (a small, shrimp-like creature).

# Epilogue

irds of prey play an important role in the natural world. By killing and eating the animals they live on, these hunters help keep populations under control. The scavengers get rid of harmful bacteria and pests by eating the "leftovers." But in spite of their strength and ferocity, birds of prey are extremely vulnerable, and they are often the first sign that we are harming our environment.

The most famous example is the use of the pesticide DDT. During the 1950s and 1960s, DDT was widely used to control pests in farm crops as well as home gardens. The pesticide, taken in by small plant-eating animals and birds, eventually entered the bodies of birds of prey that ate the smaller animals. The DDT made their eggs soft, too fragile for the young to develop properly, and birds like the Peregrine Falcon, Osprey, Bald Eagle and other raptors were facing extinction. Fortunately, some alert and concerned people made the

danger public, and the use of DDT was banned. The birds were saved, and their numbers have risen. Peregrine Falcons, like these nesting on the ledge of a building in Milwaukee (left), have been successfully reintroduced to many cities across North America.

Many birds of prey are now threatened by other pesticides and by the loss of their habitat. The Burrowing Owl (right), for example, lives in large, open areas with low vegetation, where burrows have already been dug by other animals. But human development in those areas is putting it at risk. The Spotted Owl of northwestern North America lives in the old-growth forests that are being cut down for logging and development. There are fewer Red-shouldered Hawks because of the loss of some of their forest habitat. These are only a few examples.

Although the oldest hawk on record lived thirty-eight years in the wild, the average lifespan of many hawks is only one to two years. This shows how dangerous life is for these beautiful hunters. The dangers are often from other predators or from natural periods of food shortage, but people are also to blame.

We can help keep birds of prey safe. We can continue to set aside places for birds and other animals to live unthreatened. We can be aware of how our lifestyles affect them. Most of all, we can learn about them and try to understand them. The more we know about these marvelous creatures, the better we will be able to protect them for many years to come.

# Glossary

**Air resistance:** The force of air pushing against a moving object.

**Barbed:** Having a small, sharp, backward-facing hook or series of hooks.

**Captive breeding:** Encouraging animals to reproduce in a protected habitat, for example in zoos, to help preserve the *species*.

**Carrion:** The rotted flesh of dead animals.

**Extinction:** The state of a *species* whose entire population has been wiped out, like the Passenger Pigeon.

**Falconry:** The art of hunting with birds. The bird is trained to kill and bring back the dead animal.

**Family:** A scientific term for a large grouping of birds (or other life forms) with similar characteristics. The family contains smaller sub-groups called genus, which in turn contain different *species*.

**Game bird:** A bird that is commonly hunted by humans, like quail, duck, or pheasant.

**Glide:** To fly smoothly and silently, without flapping the wings. Compare to *soar*, below.

**Incubate:** To keep eggs warm from laying until hatching, usually accomplished by the mother sitting on the eggs. If the eggs are not kept warm, the chicks will not develop.

**Invertebrate:** A class of animal with no backbone or spinal column. Includes insects, worms, shellfish, and others.

**Pesticide:** A chemical that kills unwanted pests, especially insects. It is used in gardens or on farm crops.

**Roost:** To rest or sleep on a perch. Birds may roost on a tree branch, a building beam, a telephone wire, and so on.

**Soar:** To fly high in the air. Birds often soar by flying slowly in circles high above the ground, without flapping their wings.

**Species:** Birds of the same type. These are the individual birds that we identify, like the Turkey Vulture and Martial Eagle.

**Tendons:** Bands of tough tissue that attach muscle to bone.

**Ultraviolet:** A type of light not visible to the human eye.

**Wingspan:** The distance from one wingtip to the other.

## Recommended Reading

*The Bird Almanac* by David M. Bird (Firefly Books). A guide containing facts and figures about birds from around the world.

*Birds of Prey Rescue* by Pamela Hickman (Firefly Books). Profiles the people and projects around the world that are helping endangered and threatened raptors to survive.

## Web Sites

Cornell Lab of Ornithology
www.birds.cornell.edu
Includes a field guide, complete with bird calls.

The Hawk Conservancy Trust
www.hawk-conservancy.org
Includes information about raptors from around the world.

## Acknowledgments

The authors and Madison Press Books would like to thank William McIlveen for providing research consultation. And thanks, as always, to Alex Fischer for being there whenever we need her.

Nancy Kovacs is a writer, editor, and amateur naturalist. She has done editorial work for Ontario Nature (Federation of Ontario Naturalists) and the Pontifical Institute of Mediaeval Studies Press and most recently was editor of Robert Bateman's *Backyard Birds*.

Birds of Prey was produced by
MADISON PRESS BOOKS
1000 Yonge Street, Suite 200
Toronto, Ontario, Canada M4W 2K2
**madisonpressbooks.com**

Project Editor: Carolyn Jackson
Executive Editor: Imoinda Romain
Editorial Director: Wanda Nowakowska

Art Director: Diana Sullada

Production Manager: Sandra L. Hall
Production Director: Susan Barrable

Publisher: Oliver Salzmann